Mudras  FOR Children

YOGA FOR BUSY LITTLE HANDS

Great for kids with ADD, ADHD, Autism and in Classrooms

Marsha Therese Danzig

Cover design by Sarah Barr
Book design and production by Sarah Barr
Editing by Marsha Therese Danzig
Author photograph by Rachael Kloss
Text by Marsha Therese Danzig
©2014 Marsha Therese Danzig, President, Color Me Yoga® Enterprises, LLC

Self published in the United States by Color Me Yoga® Enterprises, LLC
ISBN-10: 1495380858
ISBN-13: 9781495380853

Ordering Information: To order books and for bulk rates, please email:
info@colormeyoga.com or call 978-239-2038.

Contents

NAMASTE! WELCOME TO THE CHILDREN'S BOOK OF MUDRAS.

This book will teach you all about the wonderful world of mudras (pronounced "moo-drah"). Mudras come from India. They are also practiced in many other places, such as Thailand, Burma, and even Hawaii. They are practiced along with Yoga. Yoga combines poses, breathing, songs, meditation, prayer, relaxation and...MUDRAS!!!

WHAT IS A MUDRA?

A mudra is a symbol you make with your hands and fingers that seals the energy in your body and mind. Mudras remind you what your body, mind and spirit need.

Mudras are easy to use and loads of fun. You can practice them ANYWHERE. You can teach your friends, show your parents or your teachers, even have a mudra party. Mudras are for everybody, including you. Mudras are great. And so are you! Go for it. Do a mudra.

HOW TO USE THIS BOOK

This book is divided into six categories:

 ENERGY

 HEALING

 NATURE

 CALM

 CONFIDENCE

 SPIRIT

ENERGY mudras balance the energy in your mind, body and spirit.
NATURE mudras represent the natural world.
CONFIDENCE mudras build your self esteem.
HEALING mudras bring health and well being to your mind, body & spirit.
CALM mudras soothe and inspire you.
SPIRIT mudras awaken your awareness of your spiritual nature.

You will know each category by the symbol it has.

Next to each mudra is a letter "C" or "S". " C" means Complex (indicated by two flowers on the page). "S" means Simple (indicated by one flower on the page). You may want to keep things simple when you practice your mudras. Or you may want to have fun trying more complex mudras.

How long to practice mudras: Children ages 4-6: 1-3 minutes; Children ages 7-8: 1-5 minutes; Children ages 9-12, 1-10 minutes

WAYS TO PRACTICE MUDRAS

1. Show your friends how to chill out with mudras.

2. Do yoga mudra shadows on the wall, using a flashlight, at night at slumber parties.

3. Sneak a mudra underneath your school desk when you are feeling worried about something.

4. Share a mudra with your brother when he is annoying you.

5. Do mudras on a long drive. That way you won't need to tease your sister or bother your parents with the question "When are we going to get there?" You'll be having too much fun practicing your mudras.

6. Put down your technology. Turn off the television. Put on a mudra.

7. Do mudra show and tell for your teacher at school.

8. Impress your grandparents with Sanskrit. Sanskrit is the language of Yoga. Many mudras have Sanskrit names.

9. Bored? Try a mudra!

10. Upset about something? Do a mudra.

11. Do mudra mirrors with your friends.

12. Make your brain work for you. Do a mudra.

13. Go outside. Do a mudra right there under the sun, or even in the rain. Nature will be very happy you did.

14. Start a mudra revolution in your community. Have a mudra day to increase peace in your town or city.

15. Come up with your own unique ideas and email me, the author at: Marsha.Therese@colormeyoga.com. I will post your ideas in my newsletter.

MEET THE AUTHOR

Hi Kids. My name is Marsha Therese. I created this book. Can you guess which mudra I used to help me? Are you having fun learning these mudras? I hope so. I know I love to do mudras anytime of day. If you'd like to find out more about me, you can go to my website www.colormeyoga.com

The life in nature is the same life in me.

prana

6

imagine

My imagination is a seed in the universal garden.

apana

7

I close my eyes. It is time for me to relax.

rudra

settle

I am settled like a rock on the earth.

prithivi

9

Pow! Wow! I have lots of energy now!

✳✳

alive!

celebrate

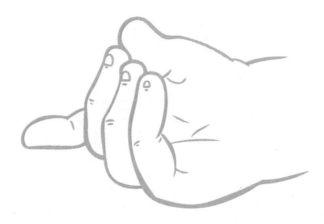

I love life!

vajra

11

I can do it!

✳✳

ganesha

inside

Inside my shell are all my precious thoughts
and feelings. I think before I speak them.

shankh

flow

I am water. Water changes. So can I.

varuna

When I feel tired, I imagine becoming an eagle,
soaring through the sky.

garuda

rest

Crocodile takes his rest to keep his energy strong.
So can I.

**

makara

persevere

I work through my problems. I never give up.

naga

secret

The secret is. . . I am perfect just the way I am.

*

pearl

open

When I open up my heart, the world listens.

padma

19

observe

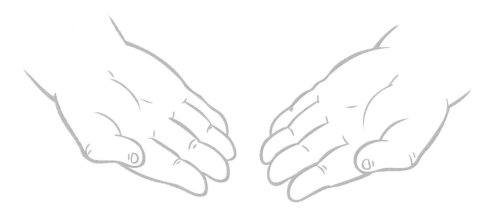

I pay attention to the beauty in life.
This is my greatest power.

✳

pushpaputa

accept

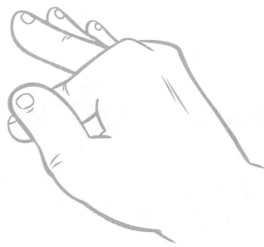

I accept myself 100%.

ahamkara

focus

I am focused and clear headed.

**

hakini

22

brave

I am brave.

bhramara

23

me

I like a lot about me.
Here's my list... fill in your list here.

kalesvara

loved

I know 100% that I am loved.

✳✳

vajrapradama

yes!

No! to negative. Yes! To positive.

✹✹

bhutadamara

know

Deep inside me I know what to do.

✱✱

i know

27

Mushti! Mushti! Mushti! I feel my anger in a way that
hurts no one, including myself.

*

mushti

28

surrender

Time to let go.

suchi

29

better

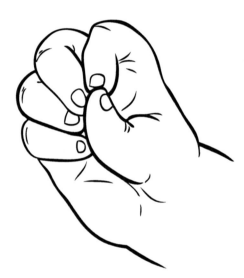

I place my fingers on any part of my body that hurts
so I can feel better.

mukula

forgive

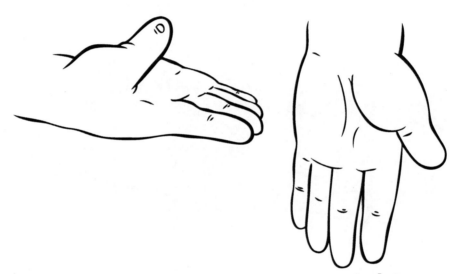

Forgiveness is important if I want to feel free.

✿✿

varada

cool

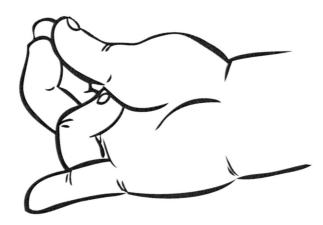

It feels good to cool down.

✤✤

mahasirs

32

wish

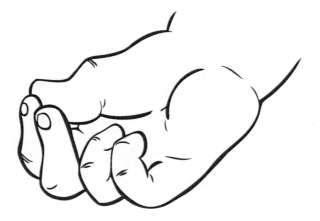

I wish, I wish, I wish... fill in the blanks.

kubera

majestic

I am calm and majestic, like a king or queen.

✿✿

matangi

quiet

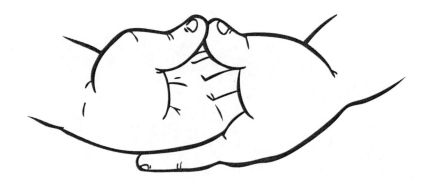

My hands hold peace and quiet.

❋❋

dhyana

listen

Steady. Strong. Breathe. Listen.

✽✽

absolute wisdom

special

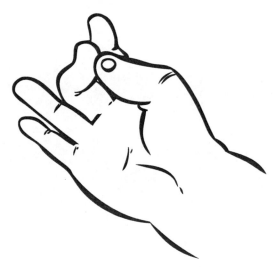

I have my own special story in the universe.

akash

infinity

My thoughts in my heart are as huge as infinity.

gyan

peace

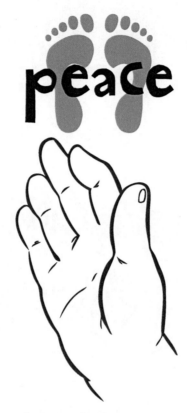

I practice peace.

abhaya

dream

When I am relaxed, I create new dreams.

uttarabodhi

sleep

I sleep peacefully.

✿✿

sakti

best

Every Day I ride my inner self train. My train knows what is best for me. The wheels are always turning.

✺✺

dharmachakra

pray

My life is a prayer of thank you.

anjali

Om, Om, oh heavenly Om is my song.

shunya

44

love

I am full of confidence, love and life.

adhi

MUDRA REMEDIES

Are you having trouble sitting still or letting your mind relax? Try Dhyana Mudra.

Do you need some refreshing new energy? Try Uttarabodhi Mudra.

Do you need to feel like you belong too? Try Ahamkara Mudra.

Are you upset with someone and need to forgive them, but it feels so hard to do? Try Abhaya Mudra.

Are you so angry you feel like punching someone but know that will hurt them and you? Try Mushti Mudra.

Do you have something important to say? Try Adhi Mudra.

Do you keep thinking about the same thing over and over?
Try Kalesvara Mudra.

Do you feel insecure today? Try Prithivi Mudra.

Do you sometimes get confused about how to balance your spiritual life and your everday life? Try Dharmachakra Mudra.

Do you want to understand your life purpose? Try Akash Mudra.

Do you have a wonderful treasure to share with the world but you feel stuck about how to share it? Try Shankh Mudra.

Do you need courage? Try Ganesha Mudra.

Do you need to let go of worries more? Try Apana Mudra.

Do you need more energy today? Try Prana Mudra.

Do you need to clear your mind AND your desk? Try Hakini Mudra.

Do you have some hearing problems? Try Shunya Mudra.

Are you having trouble staying focused today? Try Alive! Mudra.

Do you feel like everyone is telling you what to do, and it is making you confused? Try the I Know Mudra.

Are you about to try something new that scares you?
Try Vajrapradama Mudra.

Do you need to feel more inspired and less depressed?
Try Garuda Mudra.

Do you feel alone, as if no-one could ever understand?
Try Gyan Mudra with your palms up.

INDEX

28556771R00031

Made in the USA
Middletown, DE
19 January 2016